Helena

# Contents

# Introduction

## Hygge and why you should play games

Hygge is a Danish word and a way of life that values happiness, contentment, companionship and the simpler things in life above all else. It is a vital component in the lifestyle of the Danes and is part of the reason why Denmark is regarded by many as the happiest place on the planet.

There are many elements of hygge, however games and social gatherings play a fundamental role within any hygge lifestyle. We instinctively recognize the value of games for children and their development. You would have played many games yourself throughout your own childhood and perhaps you have the opportunity now to teach children those same games that you enjoyed.

We know how important games are for children, but we often fail to realize how beneficial they are for us as adults as well. Playing games, of whatever type, gives you a chance to free yourself from the stresses of work and other commitments. Games provide an opportunity to relax and socialize with friends and family, to use your imagination and creativity in all sorts of ways. Games give you a chance to play, to relax and simply to enjoy yourself.

## The benefits of game playing

We know that playing and laughter can relieve stress by the release of endorphins, the feel good chemicals that flood the body with feelings of pleasure. Playing a game, with its rules and targets and strategy is important also to help with memory and thinking skills.

Games keep you mentally sharp, as well s enhancing memory and cognitive skills. Games give us a chan e to think in different ways, to create a plan and follow a strat y to achieve a target together. Games increase our problem-s lving ability and give us confidence to handle situations tha we might not have expected to encounter. Games make us etter at thinking on our feet and adapting to different situatio s as they arise.

Physical games also promote spatial awareness and co-ordination as well as being great exercis for everyone. Games strengthen social skills such as communi ation and teamwork, as well as enhancing number and lang age skills which are required for all games.

Playing games socially forges bonds w h people as well as heightening your communication ar l teamwork skills. Relationships are strengthened when yo enjoy each other's company with games encouraging tru , co-operation with others and giving you chances to make n v friends. All of these things are key parts of a hygge lifestyle.

## What this book will give you

This book will provide you with a deta ed description of 60 games that you can use with family and iends, starting today. There are several different types of ga es that you can try. Some work best with pairs, some in large groups. Some require no equipment, some might need pen ar paper. Some games are best played around the table, some a e more suited for the outside.

I have written this book in response to many requests from readers of "How To Hygge", who were keen to know more about games and the tremendously positive effects they can have on their lifestyle. This book is an indispensable resource for anyone who is interested in games and how they can add more hygge into their daily lives.

This book is a comprehensive resource of practical ideas for games that have been tried and tested. I have played all these games myself many times and they have always proved a great hit, no matter what type of occasion or guest you have. I have played them with my own family and friends of all ages. They can be used at any time and played with anybody. All the games in this book will provide entertainment, enjoyment and fun to everyone.

The most important thing of all however is this - every single game in this book will add hygge to your life and those around you. All the games in this book create that vital sense of companionship with friends and family that is heightened through play and an enjoyable occasion spent together. They are a celebration of the simpler things in life that make us happier.

Rediscover the importance of play and the joy and happiness it can bring. Let's read on for a detailed description of 60 games that will add hygge to your life, starting today.

Helena

# Chapter 1 - Icebreaker Game

All of these games work very well in groups or large parties. These type of games work especially well to relax everyone and get people in a relaxed frame of mind for the evening. The beginning of a gathering can be a great place to introduce these games, especially if there may be a few people who are new to the group and you want to break the ice effectively.

All of these games require very little in the way of equipment – you just need friends and family and a willingness from everyone to get involved and enjoy themselves.

## Would I Lie To You?

Players: 4 or more

Equipment: None

Time: 5 minutes or more

You could play this game with 2 players, but it works best with two teams of at least 2 people each. It's even better with teams of 3 or 4. Each member of the team takes it in turn to try to tell a bizarre tale or story. It is up to the opposing team to say whether the statements are truth or a lie. They can ask questions to try and trip up the person telling the story, which might help them work out if it's fact or fiction.

You get a point for successfully guessing if the statements are true or false and the turn switches to the next team. The scores are calculated after everyone has had a go telling the truth or the lie and the highest score wins.

## Two Truths and a Lie

Players: 4 or more

Equipment: None

Time: 5 minutes or more

This is a variant of "Would I Lie To You" and is great fun at parties. It's a very good way to break the ice and get people talking. Like all good games, its rules are simple. Each person makes three statements. Two of these statements are true, the other is a lie. The group then has a discussion about the statements and their various opinions. In the end, everyone else guesses which of the statements are true and which are false.

This game doesn't have a clear winner and a loser, but it's a lot of fun and can reveal some fascinating facts about people you might never have discovered.

## Likes and Dislikes

Players: 4 or more

Equipment: None

Time: 5 minutes or more

Another simple, fun game that reveals a lot about the players. Each person writes down 3 things they like and 3 things they dislike. They don't put their name on the piece of paper, but everyone hands their papers to one person.

This person then jumbles them all up, takes each paper in turn and reads out the likes and dislikes to the whole group. It's the job of the group to try and figure out which sheet belongs to whom.

## Would you rather?

Players: 4 or more

Equipment: None

Time: 5 minutes or more

This is another enjoyable game that requires no equipment at all. Again, you can play it in small groups, but it really excels with a larger group of 8 or more. One person will ask an interesting question such as, "Would you rather go 1000 years in the future or 1000 years in the past?".

You can have either the person ask the question just of the person sitting next to them or they can go through the whole group asking each person one by one. Have a brief time limit on the answers to encourage group participation and discussion. The more imaginative the scenarios are the better this game works. You can also pose questions that offer two undesirable options or even two serious ones. You will often get some very interesting and revealing discussions as a result.

# Chapter 2 - Party Games

These games work particularly well in big groups. They will get every single person participating, working with and getting to know everyone else there. They will liven up any party and add a true hygge atmosphere to the room.

## Up Jenkins

Players: 4 or more

Equipment: A small coin

Time: 5 minutes or more

This is a good, quick game that will get everyone involved and shouting out their guesses. Split everyone into two equal sized teams and place each team on either side of the table. One person takes a coin and passes it to their teammate. This is done under the table to conceal the owner of the coin from the opposition.

The other team watches closely and when they believe they know who has the coin, one appointed member of the team will shout out, "Up Jenkins". When the other team hears this, they place their elbows on the table and raise their hands upwards. The second shout from the opposing team is, "Down Jenkins". At this point, the team with the coin slams their hands on the table, palms down.

The opposition then tries to locate which palm has the coin by knocking out all those palms which they think don't hold it. It eventually gets down to one palm which is turned over to reveal if it holds the coin or not.

## Forehead Quiz

Players: 4 or more

Equipment: Sticky Notes

Time: 5 minutes or more

This game goes around in a circle. The person to the left thinks of a famous person, fictional or real-life, and writes it on a sticky note. Then they place it on the forehead of the person to their right, so it can be seen by everyone, apart from the person guessing. The guesser can then ask a series of yes/no questions to try and work out exactly who this person on their forehead is. Whoever manages to figure out the answer with the fewest number of questions, wins.

If you want to play this with lots of people at the same time, it can be even better. Have everyone write down the name of a famous person, then place it on the forehead of the person to their right. One person now asks a question, which can only be answered with yes or no.

If the answer is "Yes", then they are allowed to ask another question. If the answer is No, then the turn passes to the next person. The winner is the person who manages to discover the identity of the person on their forehead first.

## Hidden Sayings

Players: 4 or more

Equipment: Paper

Time: 5 minutes or more

This is a fun game that takes just a little preparation, but can be hilarious throughout the evening. Before everyone arrives, prepare three pieces of paper for each guest. On each piece, write down a peculiar phrase. For example, you could try, "My shoes smell of apples" or "I like blue milk". The phrases need to be different and amusing, without being so out of the ordinary that they are immediately spotted.

Once everyone is present, tell them that the object of the game is to get these phrases into the chat while trying to make them appear to be part of everyday conversation. The winner is the person who first manages to use all three phrases without people realizing.

## 20 Questions

Players: 4 or more

Equipment: None

Time: 5 minutes or more

This is a game of deduction and logic. One person thinks of an object or a person. It can be real or fictional, but needs to be something that everyone would have a reasonable chance of knowing. Everyone then gets 20 questions to ask to try and find out what or who this thing is. The person replying can only answer "Yes" or "No". You have to be careful about your questions. At the end of the questions, you are allowed one guess for the correct answer. The turn then switches to the next person and the game continues.

## The Newlywed Game

Players: 4 or more

Equipment: Pens and Paper

Time: 5 minutes or more

This is a good game to play with couples of perhaps good friends. One person of the couple leaves the room, while the other is asked a series of questions and is asked to write down their answers. The questions might be along the lines of:

- "Where did you meet?"
- "How did you know they were the one?"
- "What did he/she think of you after your first date?"
- "What was the first Christmas present you got for each other?"
- "What are the names of his/her best friends?"

The favorites category is also a good one to try, as everyone will get to know the participants a little better as well. The questions could be:

- "What is your partner's favorite movie?"
- "What is your partner's favorite food?"
- "What is your partner's favorite book?"

Once the first person has recorded their answer, then the other half is called back in and is asked the same question. If they say the same answer as their other half did in the first round, then they gain a point. The winner is the couple with the greatest number of similar answers at the end of the game.

# Chapter 3 - Observation and Memory Games

All of these games require a little mental exertion from those playing. This might be a little tricky after the evening has progressed, but it will often lead to some very amusing results and plenty of laughter. Food, drink, good company and laughter – all good ingredients for a wonderful hygge evening.

Try these following games at your next get-together!

Memory Game

Players: 2 or more

Equipment: None

Time: 5 minutes or more

This is a simple game which will really start to test your short term memory. The first player starts off by saying, "Yesterday I went to the shops and I bought..." and then adds an item that they bought from the shop, perhaps a chocolate cake. The next person then has to repeat the phrase with the chocolate cake as well as an additional item that they add on.

The next player might say, "Yesterday I went to the shops and I bought a chocolate cake and a fishing rod". The next person then adds another item and the process repeats. The first person who forgets the sequence drops out of the game and the turn moves on to the next person. The winner is the last person left in the game.

# Action Memory Game

Players: 2 or more

Equipment: None

Time: 5 minutes or more

This is similar to the memory game where you had to remember items bought from a shop. This is changed a little now as you have to recall the actions that each person makes. If the first person touches their nose, then the second person has to touch their nose and then add an action of their own e.g. turn around. The game continues until someone forgets an action in which case they're knocked out.


# I Spy

Players: 2 or more

Equipment: None

Time: 5 minutes or more

An oldie, but a classic that is enjoyed by all. One person picks an object in the room and starts the game with, "I spy with my little eye something beginning with...". They then say the first letter of the of the object they seen. Just make sure it's something that is visible to all. You can speed up the game by adding "hot" or "cold" if people get close. The turn passes to whoever guesses the word correctly.

# Wink Murder

Players: Ideally 8 or more

Equipment: None

Time: 5 minutes or more

This is a fun game of detection. One person is nominated to be the detective. They leave the room while everyone else sits in a circle with their eyes shut. One person will then choose the murderer by silently tapping him or her on the shoulder. Everyone then opens their eyes and the detective returns to sit in the circle.

The aim of the game is for the murderer to kill as many people as he can by winking at them. Once a person sees a wink, they are to feign death and are out of the game. The aim of the detective is to figure out who the murderer is before everyone is killed.

This is a great game to be played in a decent sized group. The ideal would be around 8 to 10 people to give the detective a good chance of finding the wink murderer.


## Charades

Players: 4 or more

Equipment: None

Time: 5 minutes or more

This is a classic game that all ages can enjoy. Each person chooses a film or a book or a play or a television show for example that they act out. They are not allowed to talk and can mime particular words or even just syllables of words. The person who guesses correctly first, then has their turn miming.

You can also create a series of cards with various titles on beforehand. Each person chooses the top card and then needs to act it out. A great game that will get everyone shouting out and involved.

## Fizz Buzz

Players: 4 or more

Equipment: None

Time: 5 minutes or more

This is a great game that relies on your mental agility. It is best played at speed. The aim of the game is to try and count to 100 – with a few special exceptions. For every multiple of 3, rather than say the number, you have to say "Fizz". For every multiple of 5, instead of the number you have to say "Buzz". If the number is a multiple of both 3 and 5, you say "fizz buzz".

The beginning sequence might go like this

1, 2, fizz, 4, buzz, fizz, 7, 8, fizz, buzz and so on. People get knocked out if they make a mistake. If more than one person is still left after you get to 100, then just play on.

# Chapter 4 - Word Games

Word games are a great way to get people talking with each other and sharing their ideas. All of these games involve lots of people and will work well in any social gathering. They require very little equipment, but will also get people being highly creative, thinking on their feet and generally having a great time.

With all of these games, it is less about the winning and more about the process. The end result will be lots of laughter and a great hygge atmosphere for all.

Ghost

Players: 4 or more

Equipment: None

Time: 5 minutes or more

This is quite a tricky game, but is good fun. If you can spell, you are going to love it. One person starts the game by saying a letter. Each person then has a turn by adding a single letter to the letters that have already gone. The aim of the game is to avoid adding a letter which will make the previous letters into a word. For example, if it went D-A- and someone added the letter D, they would lose because that would spell Dad, which is a word. If they were to add the letter R, that would be fine as Dar is not a word.

Instead of adding a letter however, a player can also challenge the last player to state the word they had in mind and prove it is going to be a word. If the previous player can't name the word which begins with all the letters previous stated, then they are out of the game. If they can name the ord, then the player who challenged is out.

For example, if someone challenged D-A  , it would be fine to say it was the start of the word "Dark"   "Darling". If no-one notices a word has been formed already  r no-one challenges, the word continues to be formed and the  rns pass around.

You can play a variation of this, wh  instead of adding individual letters, you add words. The ai  is to avoid being the person who adds the last word on  which concludes a grammatically sound sentence.

## Consequences

Players: 4 or more

Equipment: Pens and Paper

Time: 5 minutes or more

This is an old classic and is perfect for pa  ies. Everyone sits in a circle with half a sheet of paper and a   n. To start the game off, each person must write an adjective   the top of the page. Then they fold over the paper and hand   to the person on the left. It is important at this point, that no-  ne else can see what has been written down. There then foll  vs a strict pattern of words which has to be written at each sta  e. Once everyone has completed that stage, then the paper  s folded again, and passed on to the left. The stages are as fo  ws:

A name of a man

An adjective

A name of a woman

Where they met

What he wore

What she wore

What he said to her

What she said to him

The consequence

What the world said about it.


At the end of all the rounds, the papers are unfolded and are read out for everyone to hear. Here's an example of how the story might have unfolded.

Anxious Jim met beguiling Wanda at a bus stop. He wore a swimming costume. Kim wore a clown suit. Jim said to Wanda, "After dinner, I like to stroll in the moonlight". She said, "I know the meaning of life"; and the consequence was they built a small restaurant on the outskirts of town. And the world said, "No surprises there then".


## Drawing consequences

Players: 4 or more

Equipment: Pens and Paper

Time: 5 minutes or more

This works on the same principle as Consequences above, but rather than using words to build a fun and imaginative story, you can only use drawings. To start, one person draws the head of a figure – it can be human or an animal. The paper is then folded over to ensure no-one else can see what has been drawn, and then passed to the next person on the left.

That person draws the torso, down to the stomach. Again, the paper is folded and handed to the next person with no-one able to see what has been drawn. The next person draws the legs of the figure, folds the paper again and passes it over. The final stage is to draw the feet. At that point, the paper is passed once more and the resulting picture is displayed for everyone to see.

## Famous Name Game

Players: 4 or more

Equipment: Pens and Paper

Time: 5 minutes or more

This is a quick and easy game that relies on a little knowledge of famous people or characters. The game starts by the first person saying the name of a famous figure. The game now moves counter-clockwise around the table with the next person required to say another name that begins with the first letter of the previous surname. For example, it might go:

Jennifer Lawrence

Lady Gaga

George Clooney

The game continues until people start to drop out when they can't think of a name fast enough. You can add another twist that the game reverses in direction if someone comes up with a name where the first name and the surname begin with the same letter e.g. Marilyn Monroe or Janet Jackson. This will keep everyone on their toes as you can be thrust back into contention very quickly!

## Name Game

Players: 2 or more

Equipment: None

Time: 5 minutes or more

A simple word game which anyone can play. One person selects a letter of the alphabet and a category. The aim of the game is to provide a word that belongs to that category and starts with that letter. For example, the category might be first names and the letter B. The answers could be "Ben" or "Bridget" or "Brian". People drop out of the game when either they can't think of another word or they repeat a word that has already been said.

## Story Game

Players: 2 or more

Equipment: None

Time: 5 minutes or more

A simple game which involves wordplay and imagination. One person starts a story with a sentence. The next person provides the first word of the next sentence. The following person provides the second, then the next provides the third and so on going round in circles. No "winner" as such, but the results are normally very funny.

## Fortunately, Unfortunately

*Play w/ Sam & Sylvia ----*

Players: 4 or more

Equipment: None

Time: 5 minutes or more

You could play this game with only two people, but it does work best with a few more. It's another game that requires a little imagination and some story telling. The first person begins with a reasonably simple statement such as "Last Monday James left home to walk to school".

The next person picks up the story with some unfortunate statement. For example, "Unfortunately he stepped into a puddle of water which went up to his chest". The next person then says something positive. For example, "Fortunately, a kind eagle swooped down and pulled James out of the puddle with his talons".

The next person then says another unfortunate event, then the next person a fortunate one and so on and so on. Again, there is no clear winner or loser as such in the game, but it gets people really using their imagination to create some funny stories.

## Teeth

Players: 4 or more

Equipment: None

Time: 5 minutes or more

This is a simple and short game. The aim of the game is to say your word without ever revealing your teeth. Everyone sits in a circle and chooses a fruit. They then tell everyone else in the group what their chosen fruit is.

A person is chosen at random to start the game. They say the name of their fruit twice, and then nominate the next person by saying their fruit twice. For example, if you chose "Apple" and it was your turn, you would say "Apple, apple" and then "Strawberry, strawberry" to hand the turn to the person who had chosen "Strawberry" previously.

The next person then needs to repeat their own chosen fruit twice and then pass on the turn by saying someone else's fruit twice. Everyone needs to watch each other and shout out if someone ever reveals their teeth. Once your teeth are shown, you are out of the game.

You can try to make people smile or laugh, but you can't touch anyone and you can't hide your teeth with anything. You can also mix this up a little by choosing a vegetable as the topic or countries or any other category you prefer.

# Chapter 5 - Pen and Paper Games

Sometimes the simple pen (or pencil) and paper can provide you with best forms of entertainment. The games in this chapter require just the most basic of equipment that you will probably have around the place anyway, but are a lot of fun and work very well in groups.

Some of these games involve drawing and you might sometimes get the protest that someone can't draw. I've played these games for many years and not once have I met someone who can't draw well enough to play. If you can draw a stick-man or a house or a ball, you can play all of these games and will enjoy them enormously.

A lot of these games are about communication and teamwork and will give people the opportunity to get to know each other a little better. The idea of sharing and helping each other while enjoying each other's company is key to hygge and these games will help promote that in your home every time you play.

## Drawing Game

Players: 4 or more

Equipment: Paper, drawing equipment, some random items

Time: 5 minutes or more

A fun game that tests the observation and description skills more than drawing. The contestants split into pairs and sit with their back to each other. One person will be doing the drawing. The other person takes a number of objects, one at a time, and describes them to their partner. They may not say what it is.

The other person needs to draw what they are hearing and say what the secret object is. You can time it to see which pair can get the most objects correct in 3 minutes.

## Things

Players: 4 or more

Equipment: Pen and Paper

Time: 5 minutes or more

You can play this game with 4 people, but the more you have the better. There's no particular winner or loser but it is a lot of fun for all the contestants of any age. The first person makes up a sentence for which everyone must write down an answer on a piece of paper. For example, they might say "Things that make you laugh" or "Things you wish you had got last birthday". Everyone writes down one response.

The person who read out the first statement collects all the pieces of paper and shuffles them. They then read out each answer to everyone else. The aim of the game is to match the statement to the person who wrote it down. It's great fun and also quite revealing of people's personality and character.

## Dots and Boxes

Players: 2 or more

Equipment: Pen and Paper

Time: 10 minutes or more

This is an easy game to learn that takes very little time to set up and minimal equipment. First draw a rectangle of dots on a piece of paper. It will finish looking something like this for a 3x3 grid:

.     .     .

.     .     .

.     .     .

Now each person takes it in turn to draw a line, horizontal or vertical, between two adjacent dots. They must be next to each other and you can't go diagonally across. If you are the player who completes the box, then you have won that box and you put your initials inside it. The aim of the game is to prevent situations where you end up giving your opponent an easy way to capture a box. The player with the greatest number of captured boxes, once every line has been filled in, is the winner.

## Battleships

Players: 2

Equipment: Pen and Paper

Time: 15 minutes or more

A great game to play which is full of logic and deduction. Each player draws a 10x10 grid on their sheet. The grids have columns which are numbered 1 to 10 and rows which are from A to J. On the grid in front of them, the player draws rectangles which signify some type of sea-faring vessel. You can mix up the number and type of vessels you can draw, but to start with a good configuration is as follows.

1 Aircraft Carrier – the biggest of all, this occupies 5 squares

1 Battleship – a little smaller at 4 squares

1 Cruiser – smaller still – 3 squares long

2 Destroyers – these are 2 squares

2 Submarines, the hardest to find as they are 1 square each

The vessel can be drawn horizontally or vertically and cannot be split across squares. The vessels cannot overlap.

To play the game, each person calls out a co-ordinate e.g. A4 or C5 which corresponds to a particular grid location. The opponent then signifies whether this is a hit or not by shouting out "hit" or "miss". Once every square of a vessel has been struck, then the vessel sinks and its demise is announced by the player. Each grid location is recorded on the paper with an X for a hit and a O for a miss.

The winner is the first person to successfully sink all of the opponent's fleet. You can mix it up a little by telling your opponent what type of boat has been hit so it's easier to work out where to go next.


Word Countdown


Players: 2 or more

Equipment: Pen and Paper

Time: 15 minutes or more

Another game that is fun and improves word skills. Each player takes it in turn to call out a letter which is recorded on the piece of paper. Nine letters are required for each game. The aim of the game now is to try and work out what the longest possible word is that can be made from these 9 letters. So if you had,

D A C I N O C R O

One person could call out CORD and the other might come up with ACCORD. In that case, the second player would win 6 points and the opponent 0. If both players have the same number of letters, they get the same number of points. A special case is when someone uses all the letters, in which case they get 18 points. For the word above you could have had ACCORDION for 18 points. You can play either a set number of rounds or the first person up to a score.


## Pictionary


Players: 4 or more

Equipment: Pen and Paper

Time: 15 minutes or more

This is best played in two teams. Beforehand, write down a number of phrases, one per piece of paper, and fold them up so no-one can see what was written down. One person from the team is going to be the artist and the rest of the team need to guess what word or phrase is being drawn. Place all the pieces of paper in a hat or a bowl. The artist takes a paper randomly and draws the phrase as quickly as they can. Give each artist a minute so the team can guess as many as possible.

You can play until everyone has had a turn drawing or a previously agreed winning target has been met. You can also have various categories of phrase to mix up the game as well.

## Tic-Tac-Toe

Players: 2

Equipment: Pen and Paper

Time: 5 minutes or more

Perhaps the best known paper game there is, but it couldn't go without a mention. Two horizontal lines are drawn and then two vertical lines which go through the horizontal ones producing a grid of 9 boxes. One player gets to draw an X, the other a O. The aim is to get three of your symbol in a row, either vertically, horizontally or diagonally.

## Hangman

Players: 2

Equipment: Pen and Paper

Time: 5 minutes or more

Another classic pen and paper game that adds elements of word play as well as a rather vicious premise. The rules are simple. One player thinks of a word and then puts down a series of horizontal lines which represent the number of letters in the word. They also draw a gallows above the lines.

All the remaining players now take it in turns to call out letters. If they identify a letter that is contained in the word, then the blank (or blanks if the letter repeats) are filled in. If they say a letter that is not within the word, then a body part is added to the victim of the gallows. You can play to as many body parts as you like, but at a minimum you should add the head, torso, two arms and two legs. Once the man is fully drawn, the game is over and the artist wins.

You can make it trickier for those guessing, by going for short words and ones which don't contain common letters. Most people will go for E, R, S or T so any word without those in give you a good chance of drawing the full hang man!

## Password

Players: 4 or more in two teams

Equipment: Pen and Paper

Time: 5 minutes or more

This is another team game, based around words, that requires a little thought and collaboration. If you are hosting, then before everyone arrives prepare the rounds. Each round needs five "passwords" based around a particular theme of your choosing.

Each team nominates one person who will give their team-mates clues about the word. Each clue can be only one-word long. If the team fails to guess what the word is, then the turn passes over to the opposition. Each team gets three clues to guess what the password is. If a team guesses what the password is, they are then given one shot at guessing what the overall theme is.

To ensure fairness, no-one is allowed to state the word or give two word clues or use a foreign language to describe the password. You can't act it out or speak in way that might give it away either.

The scoring is simple. You get one point per password that is guessed correctly. If you guess what the theme is after one attempt, you get an extra 5 points. After two clues, you get 4 points. Three clues, you get 3 points, 4 clues earn you 2 points and if it takes 5 points, your team will earn just the one extra point.

You can play as many rounds as you wish or stop once a pre-agreed target is met. If you don't fancy making up the themes and password yourself, you can have each team create them for the opposition. You can check them over to make sure they are fair and not too difficult.

This is a lot of fun and will lead to discussion and working together as a team to solve the passwords.

## Sprouts

Players: 2

Equipment: Pen and Paper

Time: 5 minutes or more

This looks like the simplest game you can think of and its rules are disarmingly easy to understand. Tactically, however it is complex and can take a good deal of thinking about. To start with, you will need some paper with a few dots drawn on it. The aim of the game is to draw a line from one dot to another dot. It doesn't matter if the line is curved or straight but it may not pass through another line.

Somewhere along the new line a dot is placed, but the new dot can't be on top of a previously existing dot. You may create a line from one dot back to itself. However, no dot is allowed to have more than 3 lines coming out of it.

The winner is the player who makes the last available move. Despite sounding reasonably easy, this is a game that has considerable complexity and will leave you scratching your head as you try and figure out the best move!


## Paper Connect 4

Players: 2

Equipment: Pen and Paper

Time: 5 minutes or more

You may have played Connect 4 previously with equipment, but it's equally easy to play just on pen and paper. Construct a 10x10 grid on a piece of paper. Each person then takes it in turn to draw either an X or a O. The winner is the person who connects 4 in a row. The row can be horizontal, vertical or diagonal. It's a great game of strategy and tactics, that rewards a little lateral thinking.

# Chapter 6 - Card Games

A pack of only 52 cards is able to provide a wonderful array of games that can be enjoyed by all ages. All of the games I have described below are simple to explain to a group and you can get started within five minutes. They also allow a deeper strategy once you become a little more experienced with the game.

The games here are great to promote social interaction as well as numerical and logic skills. They encourage conversation, can be played at a good speed and give everyone at the table a chance to get involved and emerge victorious. Some of these games will become firm favorites to be played many times over the years to come and will bring a lot of joy and fun into any social gathering.

## Go Fish

Players: 2 or more

Equipment: Deck of cards

Time: 5 minutes or more

This is a very entertaining game that can be played by all ages. The cards are dealt according to the following rules. If you are playing just with 2 or 3 players, then each player will get 7 cards. Any more players, then each player gets 5 cards.

The leftover cards become the "pond" in a pile on the table in front of everyone. The first person to the left of the dealer goes first. They can ask any other player if they have a card, but the same rank of card must also be held in their hand. For example, if they have an Ace, they can ask for an Ace from whomever they wish. If they have a 6, they can ask for a 6 from anyone. If they didn't have a Queen however, they couldn't ask for a Queen.

If the person being asked, has the card then they must hand over that card to the person asking for it. If they don't have the card, then they say "Go Fish". The person who asked then has to pick a card up from the pond in front of them and the turn passes to the next person on the left. Once a person has four of a kind, they place those cards face-up in front of them. The aim of the game, is to get rid of all of your cards within a 4 card set

## Crazy 8s

Players: 2 or more

Equipment: Deck of cards

Time: 5 minutes or more

Another quick-fire game where the aim is to get rid of every card you have. Each player is dealt 5 cards to start with. The remaining cards are placed in the middle, face down. The top card is then removed and placed faced up next to the existing pile (if it's an 8, put it in a random location and choose again).

Play starts with the first person to the dealer's left. They need to place a card on top of the face-up card. It needs to be either the same suit as the face-up card or the same number. For example, if it were the 4 of Spades facing upwards, then you could place any spade or any of the other 4s (clubs, diamonds, hearts) on top. If they don't have any cards that can be placed down, then they need to carry on picking up cards until one matches the face-up card.

At some point, the pile will run out. When this takes place, play passes to the next player and the deck (without the topmost card) is shuffled. The card that was previously face up becomes the new starting card next to the deck.

The exception to the rules is the magic 8 card. If a player has any 8, they can place this no matter what card is showing. Because it's wild they also need to nominate a suit of their choosing. You win once all your cards have disappeared onto the deck!

## Concentration

Players: 2 or more

Equipment: Deck of cards

Time: 5 minutes or more

This is sometimes played with a special deck of cards, but a normal pack is perfectly fine to use. This is a good game of memory and focus – you certainly need a little concentration to win. All the cards from a deck are placed face down on the table or on the floor. You will need a good sized space for this game. The cards can either be in a particular grid format or completely in a random location.

Each player is allowed to choose two cards. Each choice involves picking a card and turning it face up so everyone can see. The aim is to get as many matching pairs as possible. You are looking for 2 8s or 2 Kings or whatever paid you can find. If you do manage to get a pair, then you get another go.

If you don't pick out a pair, then both the cards are turned over in their original location. The aim is to try and watch and remember where each card is, so you can get a lot of pairs as the game wears on. The game is over when all the cards have been picked up. The winner is the person with the most pairs.

If you wanted to make it a little harder, you can insist that a pair must match both in color and in number. For example, the match to the 4 clubs is the 4 of spades. The 4 of diamonds and hearts would make a separate pair. This makes the game a little trickier and longer to play, but can be really good for older players.

## Rummy

Players: 2 - 6

Equipment: Deck of cards

Time: 5 minutes or more

This is an absolute classic of a card game that my family has played for years. It's easy to learn the rules, yet can also be quite tactical as well. It is always a lot of fun to play.

The aim of this game is get rid of your cards by creating melds. A meld can be either a set of three or four cards of the same number (for example, 3 Kings or 3 9s) or a run which is when you have three or more of the same suit in sequence (for example the 3, 4 and 5 of Hearts). For the purposes of a run, note that an Ace is low (so below a 2, not above a King) and you're not allowed to "wrap around" (you can't have Queen, King, Ace, 2 for example).

If there are just two of you, then start with 10 cards each. If there are 3 or 4, then deal each player 7. If there are 5 or 6 players, then each player should get 6 cards. Having dealt all the cards, place the deck face down on the table. Turn the top card over, so you can see what it is, and place it next to the deck.

The game starts with the first player to the left of the dealer taking either the face-up card or a card from the deck. The player can then put down any meld they have on the table. You can put down more than one if you have that as well.

As the game progresses, you can then place any remaining cards you have on melds that currently exist on the table as long as they fit. If there were 3 Jacks on table as a meld, you could add your Jack to the meld as well. If there was a run of 3, 4 and 5 of Spades and you had either the 2 or 6 of Spades, you could put that down as well.

Your turn ends by placing one card on the discard pile. You are not allowed to discard the same card you just picked up though. If the card you lay on the discard pile is your final card, then you win. If you place all your cards on the table through melds, then you win as well. If the deck runs out before anyone has won, then shuffle the cards in the deck and go again.

The scoring for Rummy is simple. If you have won the round, you are the only player to gain points. All the cards that the other players have are collected. If they have any face cards, each of those is worth 10 points. An ace is 1 point. The other cards are simply their value (for example, a 6 is worth 6 points). You can make your own target of course for the winner but we normally play to 200 points.

There is a bonus score if you manage to Go Rummy. This means you put down all of your cards, for the first time, in one go. It must be the very first time you lay down any cards. The reward for this rather risk move is that you will get double the amount of points.

## Slapjack

Players: 4 or more

Equipment: Deck of cards

Time: 5 minutes or more

This is a very simple game. It's not particularly tactical but it is fast and fun and will get everyone moving and into the game. Deal the deck evenly to all the players.

Each player keeps their cards in front of them face down so not even they can see what the cards are. The first person to the left of the dealer places a card in the middle of the table.

The next person places a card on top of that card. Play continues in the same way until a Jack appears. At that point the first person to place their hand over the cards wins all of them and adds them to the bottom of their own pile.

The chances are lots of people will attempt to go for the cards so it's the player whose hand is at the bottom of the pile who wins. If someone makes a mistake and slaps the deck when it's not a Jack, they have to give their top card to the dealer.

You can still have a go even if you run out of cards by trying to slap a Jack when it appears on top of the pile.

The winner is the person who ends up with the entire deck!

## I Doubt It

Players: 3 or more

Equipment: Deck of cards

Time: 5 minutes or more

This is a game of trickery and bluff where fooling your opponents will lead to victory. The rules are very simple however. The cards are dealt evenly to all the players. The player to the left of the dealer starts by laying down a card or cards on the table and saying how many aces there are. The next player does the same but with 2s. The next player does the same again but with 3s and so on until you get to the Kings and the process starts again with Aces. You can also pass your turn.

Of course, as you place the cards face down, you are able to bluff as well. If a person doesn't believe you are telling the truth, then they call out, "I doubt it". If the person was bluffing, they have to pick up all the cards that have been discarded so far. However, if the person wasn't bluffing the person who shouted out has to pick up all the cards.

The winner will be the person who gets rid of their cards first!

## Go Boom!

Players: 3 or more

Equipment: Deck of cards

Time: 5 minutes or more

A fun game that is fast and loud to play in a good sized group. Each player is dealt 7 cards, with the rest of the pack face down in the middle. The player to the left of the dealer goes first and is allowed to play any card from their hand.

The next player now needs to play a card that is the same suit as the first card or the same number. For example, if it were the 3 of Clubs, you could follow with any club or the 3 of Diamonds, Hearts or Spades.

If the next player can't lay a card down from their hand, then they must pick one up from the face down pack, until they can play. If there are no cards left to pick up, then that player has to pass.

The winner is the first person to get rid of all their cards. You can play it just as a round system, but the scoring is easy too. Just add up the value of the cards that remain in all the other players' hands. An ace is 1, while all the face cards are 10. The rest of the cards are just worth their rank (3, 4, 8, etc.).

## Chapter 7 - Board Games

Board games are a great way to promote hygge within your home. They work really well at getting everyone involved in an activity together, communicating with each other and generally enjoying each other's company.

When you are heavily involved in a board game, you are necessarily dedicating yourself to the activity. Your focus and attention is on what is in front of you now, in the moment. Distractions from work via a computer or a cell phone are removed and you are able to immerse yourself in good company and an enjoyable activity.

Board games work very well for a hygge afternoon, with the candles blazing and a good cup of tea with a slice of cake. They're a great way to get large groups involved, having fun and engaging together. Below are some of my family's favorite games for you to try.

## Boggle

This is a wonderful game that is great for word and language skills. It consists simply of a plastic grid into which 16 wooden dice sit. A lid is placed over the top and the letters are shaken around to produce a different random configuration each time. Rather than numbers, each side displays a letter. The aim of the game is to get as many words as possible from the letter dice. The letters can't be repeated and they must be next to each other in some way – horizontal, vertical or diagonally.

We normally play a minimum of 3 or sometimes 4 letter words for adults, but you can lower that requirement to 2 for younger children. Each round is quick and everyone will contribute their words at the end. A great game to get people talking as well as learning new words.

## Trivial Pursuit

An old game, but one that is continually updated with various versions and different questions. We normally play this as two or sometimes three teams, as you get more right and there is less of an interval between turns which makes it more interesting. This is another game that will get people communicating within a team and scratching their head trying to get to the answer.

## Scrabble

I love Scrabble and have enjoyed many evenings playing this in front of the fire. We normally play with 4 players. It can take a couple of hours at times as people get quite tactical with their choice of letters and where they are going to put them, but it's great fun for a more slow-paced, relaxed game that relies on word play. You will get to know a lot of very rare two and three letter words as well!

## Balderdash

This might be seen as a combination of various other games and is lots of fun, especially if you enjoy word games. The game works by one person reading one some very rare and exotic word that no-one will have a clue what it means. Everyone else than writes down their own definition of the word and all of them, including the correct one are read out by the first person.

Then people vote for what they think is the correct answer. You get points if people vote for your definition or if you vote correctly yourself. Lots of fun and gets people talking and laughing about some of the definitions that get written.

## Carcassonne

This is a game played with tiles which can be played by up to five players. There are lots of various expansion packs for it, if it becomes popular in your family and you want to try something new. This isn't the easy game to get to grips with when you start, but it does reward concentration and tactics and will have its dedicated followers in most households.

## Pandemic

This is a really interesting one because you need to play together so that everyone wins. It has a maximum of four players and each person plays a specialist role in preventing diseases spreading throughout the world. Various packs are available as well if you want to try a new variation, but playing a co-operative game is quite different from playing against each other and makes a good change. It is highly tactical though, so will require focus and concentration to win!

## Uno

Every household needs to have this game. This is a classic game that plays along the same lines as Crazy 8s (see above). It looks great, it plays quickly and everyone can pick up the rules very easily. A great game to play in a large group.

## Dobble

It's not a board game I know, but I couldn't not include Dobble. Very simple to play, it's a great game of observation and reflexes. It consists of cards with various symbols on. Each card is different and is used in various ways for the mini-games. It's fast, action-paced and everyone in the family will enjoy it. A must.

## Say Anything

This is a lot of fun in groups again. For each round someone is chosen to the Judge. The judge then draws a card and asks the question on it. It might say, for example, "What would be the best thing to do on the moon?". Everyone then writes down an answer and displays it to the group.

The judge chooses their favorite response, but doesn't tell anyone. The aim of the game is to nominate which answer the Judge chose.

This is a beautiful game that now has various versions. You need to collect various cards that will allow you to connect different places via train lines. Like all great games, the rules are very simple to understand, but figuring out the best tactics is not so easy. It looks and feels great to play though and a good game can take about an hour. You can play with as few as 2 players, but I find it works better with 4 or 5.

All of these games are great to play in groups and will encourage participation, talking together and generally a lot of laughter and fun. They can be played in various age groups, perhaps with some rule modifications for much younger children, but generally the more that play the better.

# Chapter 8 - Outdoor Games

Although the weather might not be great all the time during the winter months, there will still be opportunities to get outside and enjoy some fresh air. Even if you have to rug up with appropriate winter wear, it's always important to engage in some kind of physical exercise to get the circulation going and the blood pumping through the body.

It's re-invigorating and will leave you feeling you like you have well and truly earned your hot drink and cake to come. Here are a few games that children will love to engage in, no matter what time of year it is.

## Hide and Seek

Players: Any

Equipment: None

Needs very little explanation as you have probably played it many times yourself previously. You can mix it up a little by changing the amount of time people have to hide or add a time limit to how long the finder has. A great game that can appeal to all ages.

## Capture the Flag

Players: 8 or more

Equipment: A large space, something to make a line and 2 objects to represent the flag

This is so much fun to play with large groups. You need to split everyone into two teams and will need at least 4 people per team for a good game. Take a large area and divide it into two. You can use whatever you have to hand to mark out the territory of each team. Hide an item somewhere in each team's territory.

The aim for each team is to sneak into the enemy territory, grab their flag and bring it back into their own territory. However, if a member of the opposition tags you, then you are imprisoned. You can only be released when a member of your own team tags you, at which point you can run away or attack again. It's quite an interesting game to watch as well – it's frenetic but can also get quite tactical at times too.

## Hopscotch

Players: Any

Equipment: Some chalk and a small pebble

Another traditional game that can be played by all ages and is great exercise as well. If you have the equipment, you can also play this inside though it is more commonly associated with the outdoors. Construct a hopscotch grid, numbering each square up to 10. Find a small pebble and throw it onto the first square. Now comes the hard part.

Hop over the pebble, using one foot or two depending on the pattern you have made, right to the end (you can rest at the end) and then back again to Square 2. On one foot, bend down, pick up the pebble in the first square and go back to the start. Now do the same again, but try and hit square 2 with your pebble. If you miss the next square, then the next person has their turn. The winner is the first person to complete all the squares.

## Simon Says

Players: Any

Equipment: None

You don't need to be outside to play this of course, but you might find it a little easier if there are big numbers and lots of physical actions going on. This is a simple game that can be good fun, especially when played at speed – it certainly tests powers of concentration. One person is Simon.

This person will start by saying something like, "Simon says touch your feet". As the sentence started "Simon says", then everyone should do the action. However, if Simon does not start a sentence with "Simon says", then the actions should be ignored.

If anyone does follow the action without "Simon" being mentioned, then they are out of the game. The winner is the last person left standing.

# Jump Rope and Double Dutch

Players: 3 or more

Equipment: Long skipping rope

This is an entertaining game that also happens to be extremely beneficial for your health. It's a great form of exercise, that will soon leave you out of breath. A little practice will see your stamina increase soon enough however.

I've said 3 players above, but of course this is also a game you can do by yourself if you just fancy the exercise. See how many you can do in 30 seconds or how long you can keep it up without stopping. Once you get proficient, you can add in some tricks such as crossing over your arms or swinging from the sides.

The game really comes into its own as entertainment once you get more people involved however. Get a longer rope with two people at either end spinning it over the person in the middle. If the rope is long enough, you can have more than 1 in the middle as well. If you want to step it up a little further, then add in another rope to go double dutch.

Each person at the end now holds one rope in each hand and spins them in opposite directions. This is very fast and you have to be quite agile to be able to time it correctly, but it's great after practice and is a lot of fun.

Add a competitive element to it by counting the number of times each person manages to jump successfully before catching the rope. You can also sing songs while doing which can add to the rhythm of the game to help the jumper.

## Giant Tumble Tower

Players: 2 or more

Equipment: Large building blocks

There are a few versions of this game around. It is essentially a giant Jenga that is designed to be played outside. The stacks can get high at over 5 feet, so it may not be suitable for children of all ages, especially when the blocks fall, but it's fun game that tests co-ordination and spatial awareness. The wooden blocks have a lovely, textured, tactile feel as well. If you're good with your hands and you have the right equipment you can build your own set as well. Enjoy painting the blocks different colors for another fun activity that everyone can enjoy.

## Horseshoes

Players: 2 or more

Equipment: Horseshoe game

A classic that is always fun to play for everyone. Set it up in the garden on a summer day and you can be guaranteed everyone will want to join in. Customize your own set with decorations and different colors as you see fit for an added touch of hygge.

## Water Bombs

Players: 2 or more

Equipment: Water balloons or sponges

On a hot summer day, there is little more refreshing then stocking up with your stash of water balloons and hurling them at the opposition. This is clearly a summer activity, but lots of fun. You can also get little water sponges rather than the traditional balloon form, if you don't want to pick up all the bits at the end of the day.

## Marbles

Players: 2 or more

Equipment: A set of marbles and some chalk

To play marbles you will first need to set up a circle on a flat piece of ground. We normally go for one that's about 2 to 3 feet in diameter. Draw two lines, opposite each other, outside the circle. The players are not allowed to get any closer to the circle or it will be too easy. To get started, each player rolls their marble to the other line and whoever is closest goes first.

Add the marbles into the center of the circle. It really doesn't matter how many you use, but an odd number is better to guarantee a winner. The first person now kneels down, rests their knuckles on the grass and flicks out the marble from the first with their thumb. It's customary to use a slightly bigger marble for this first throw called a shooter, but if they're all the same size, that's fine as well.

If any marbles are knocked outside the circle with the first throw, then the thrower keeps them. They also go again, and repeat the process wherever their shooter finished. When the first person eventually fails to knock a marble out of the circle, they must leave their shooter where it finished and the turn moves to the next player.

The next player shoots from behind the line again. If a shooter is then knocked out somewhere, its owner must shoot from that position next time. The shooter marble does not pass to the opposition. The second player continues until they fail to knock a marble out, at which point play passes to the next person. The whole process repeats until all the marbles have been knocked out of the circle. The winner is the person with the most marbles left in their possession.

# Conclusion

Games are an essential part of hygge and I hope this book has given you plenty of inspiration for all types of games that can be played with family or friends or even with people you have just met.

Games are vital for our well-being, especially when played with others, giving us a chance to relax, a time to socialise and an opportunity to forge relationships with all sorts of people.

As children, we are taught games at a very early age, as the importance of interaction and being together with other people is recognized. We know that games provide great mental stimulation and allow us to think about both short and long term strategy, exercising parts of the brain that may lay dormant for most of the day. All of this is an important part of staying mentally healthy and sharp throughout our life.

Many of the games in the book also have a physical element as well, allowing us to exercise and get outside where and when we can, even in the dark winter. A big part of hygge is about being warm and comfortable within your environment, but hygge still involves exercise and remaining fit.

Getting outside in the fresh and cold air and exerting ourselves is an essential part of the winter regime and will make coming back home to the warm even more satisfying and enjoyable.

The games outlined in this book have provided you with a great range of games from the mental to the physical, to games for pairs to large groups, from games with no equipment to those that need a special board and pieces.

All of them however, will provide you with a chance to have fun and to enjoy yourself. Ultimately, that is the main reason for all of us to play. Playing games reminds us of the pleasure of the company of others and all the positive emotions we feel when we are surrounded by friends and family. That is true hygge.

Happy game playing!


Helena

## More Books by the Author

I very much hope you have enjoyed reading this book and will continue to do so for many years to come. I have a small favor to ask of you myself – could you take just one minute to leave me a review at amazon?

It would really help me to reach new readers and would me a lot to me personally. Thank you very much for your time.

If you are interested in learning more about hygge, all of its positive benefits and how you can make it part of your own life today, then please have a look at the other books I have written below. I hope you enjoy reading them!

How To

# HYGGE

## 33

WAYS TO LEAD A HAPPY, HEALTHY
AND CONTENTED LIFE THROUGH
THE DANISH ART OF HYGGE

HELENA OLSEN

# HYGGE
## *Habits*

**42** HABITS FOR A HAPPY LIFE
THROUGH DANISH HYGGE THAT
TAKE FIVE MINUTES OR LESS

## HELENA OLSEN

.

Made in the USA
Middletown, DE
20 December 2019

81563035R00033